The History of Soccer

Gain a New Appreciation for Soccer through Its History, Evolution, and Development into the Sport It Is Today

by Jessie Perault

Table of Contents

Introduction

By far the world's most popular sport, soccer – also known as "association football" – exists today as a multi-billion dollar industry.

Truly the world's sport of choice, it has some 250 million registered players in more than 200 of the world's countries. That's a quarter of a billion active players doing their bit to contribute to the long history of soccer. Almost as popular as the game itself, idolized soccer stars, with their huge salaries, fast cars and at times even the soccer WAGS (wives and girlfriends) steal a lot of the limelight away from the on-field action.

The most popular format of the game is association football or association soccer, which is the "official" game as it's played between two teams of eleven players each on an outdoor field. This official format alone tops the list of the most popular sports in the world, with a global fan base totaling half of the world's entire population. What has been fondly cited as the "Beautiful Game," however, transcends the formalized 11-v-11 association format, with futsal (indoor soccer on a smaller field) with only 5 players on each side, and freestyle soccer forming a small part of its many variations.

A lot of elements contribute to what makes soccer the world's most beloved sporting code, including (but definitely not limited to) the sheer simplicity of the game and what the supremely skilled players can turn that simplicity into — insane, passion-igniting moments of atheltic brilliance that fans can't stop talking about for weeks, to be remembered forever in the sport's ever developing history.

We could analyze and discuss the greatest players and teams to have ever played the game or we could draw inspiration from all the David-versus-Goliath upsets which only serve to add to the brilliance of the Beautiful Game, but perhaps what makes soccer the sport it is today is its fascinating and glorious history. And that's exactly what this particular book is about — exploring the vast and rich history of soccer, the evolution of the game along with interesting historical events which contributed to the game as it exists today.

Read on to gain a new appreciation for the game of soccer as we shine a spotlight on its very early (and often disputed) beginnings, its contemporary history as a formalized sport, how money affected the course of the game's history, and what the records reveal about the game's super-powers.

A game which has managed to touch the lives of half of the world's entire population has history that extends far beyond the field, so expect interesting off-field (but related) historical facts and stories within these pages as well. Of course an attempt to cover the entire history of soccer in detail would require an entire set of encyclopedias, a dedicated museum, and a dynamically expanding cloud-storage server, so our focus will be limited to only the most pertinent and interesting events that have formed this incredible sport.

Chapter 1: The (Disputed) Origins of Soccer

People have entertained themselves and onlookers by kicking a ball around for a very long time. The art of ball-control dates back thousands of years, with the considerable measure of skill required to maintain control of the ball using one's feet forming the basis of the world's fascination with the game.

The exact origins of soccer are vociferously debated and widely disputed, largely because there is evidence of a variety of very early games which are thought to have contributed to the sport as we know it today. Association football (soccer) as it is played today boasts a contemporary history extending beyond a century, with 1863 seeing the formation of the Football Association (FA). Eleven schools and clubs from London congregated to form a uniform set of rules to govern all soccer matches played between them. This meeting was held on October 26th at the Freeman's Tavern, which perhaps serves as the genesis of what is now a very advanced tradition of weekend soccer viewing at many pubs in the UK and across the world, although television had yet to be invented at that particular time. The very first soccer match governed by these new laws played out to a goalless (0-0) draw, when Barnes Football Club took on Richmond Football Club on December 19th 1863. The match took place at Barnes Common, a common land located in South East Barnes, London.

While today's modern game is indeed attributed to that 1863 Freeman's Tavern meeting in London, evidence of the earliest form of a soccer-like game dates all the way back to the Chinese Han Dynasty. During the period spanning 5000 to 300 B.C, a game known as "Ts'u Chü" or "Cùjū" (蹴鞠) was played as an exercise documented in a military manual. The exercise seemed to have numerous variations, one of which disallowed players from aiming at their target unobstructed.

Like modern-day association soccer, the players were only allowed to use their feet, chest, shoulders and even their backs to control the ball. The majestic skill of a certain Ronaldinho comes to mind as the only instance where a player actually used their back in the modern game though, during a full professional match for Barcelona Football Club! The ancient game of Ts'u Chü had an element of excessive physicality to it since players had to try and stave off the unwelcomed attacks from their counterparts while trying to kick the leather ball (stuffed with hair) into a net woven between two posts. "Ts'u Chü" literally translates to "kick [the] ball with [your] feet," so this early Eastern version bears more than a passing resemblance to the game known as soccer and zúqíu (足球) today.

Between 500 and 600 years later, Kemari emerged as another version of the game played in Japan. Kemari is still popularly played to this day, making use of a footbag, which is also another name for the game ("playing footbags"). "Hacky Sacks" is yet another variation in the name of what is known as Kemari in Japan, although Hacky Sack is a specific trademark of a footbag manufacturer.

Kemari differed from Ts'u Chü in that it wasn't quite as competitive. The objective in Kemari is to keep the ball in the air while skillfully passing it around between players standing in a circle, with limited space. Everybody is essentially in the "same team" and there's no competition for possession of the ball. Kemari clearly has strong connections with what is known as "keepy-uppy" in the modern game, where players simply try to keep a modern day, official-sized soccer ball from hitting the ground while passing it around between them. It has been suggested that the art of freestyling (freestyle soccer) also owes its existence to the ancient Japanese game of Kemari.

In 611 A.D. Japanese Kemari players had the equivalent of an international match against Chinese Ts'u Chü players, each team essentially showcasing their own version of the game. This 611 A.D. date marks a definite occurrence of this "international" match, but it is believed that a much earlier match of exactly the same kind took place around 50 B.C.

There are numerous other historical games which could possibly have contributed to the formation of the game of soccer, although some of these hardly involved the use of feet. The tomb of ancient Egyptian Great Chief of the Oryx, Baqet III (2500 B.C.) features images of a ball-game which seems to have been played by young women, although no details of its actual rules have been recovered. Ancient Greece also had a game known as "Episkyros," while ancient Rome is known for their game of "Harpastum."

1600 A.D., dating all the way back to 600 A.D., featured a game played in Central America and Mexico. The game was played on a deep-set court which was 40 to 50 feet in length. The objective was to get the rubber ball through a wooden or stone ring mounted in the center of each wall.

In Canada and Alaska (1600), a game known as Aqsaqtuk (football on ice) was enjoyed by the native Inuit. The balls used were stuffed with moss, grass, and caribou hair and there the legend of the game lives on, which lays claim to a couple of villages that played against each other using goal posts no less than ten miles apart.

Native American Indians in the original settlement of Jamestown (1620) engaged in a game known as "Pasuckuakohowog," which literally translates to "they congregate to play ball with the foot." This was a very rough game and was outrageous in many ways. The number of players participating reached as many as a thousand at any time, with goals that were a mile apart. The field was half a mile in width, housed on the beach.

While the most recognizable form of what is now known as soccer can be traced back to its 1863 origins in London, the earliest football games were played within the British Isles in the 700s. East England is also thought to contribute to the game following a popular story in which the Danish Prince's severed head was kicked around, soon after his defeat in a war. Like the Native American Pasuckuakohowog game, violence was the order of the day to the extent that injuries and even deaths were quite common.

England's Eton College established a set of laws by which the game was to be played by their house teams (1815). 1848 saw a further standardization of the rules, with the subsequent version of the game assumed by all participating schools, colleges and universities. These new standardized laws were referred to as the Cambridge Rules of football.

The game would go on to take several forms between 1848 and 1863, with many players still diverting very far from the Cambridge Rules of football. Soccer (football), Gaelic football and rugby football were all variations of the game still loosely referred to as football (soccer), but by the end of the 18th century, soccer (football) started to get explicitly separated from games which resembled rugby (like Gaelic football), or American and Australian rules football-type games.

Following the historic 1863 formation of the Football Association, the penalty kick was introduced in 1888. It wasn't until Fédération Internationale de Football Association (FIFA, or the International Federation of Association Football) was established that soccer grew in leaps and bounds to become a global institution. Delegates from Belgium, Denmark, France, the Netherlands, Spain, Sweden, and Switzerland congregated in Paris, on May 21st 1904 and what is still recognized as the highest authority in world soccer was formed.

Chapter 2: Soccer's Global Growth

Soccer's first real entry into the global big-time came four years prior to the formation of FIFA, when soccer tournaments were played in the 1900 Olympic Games. 30 years later, in 1930, the first FIFA World Cup was held in Montevideo, Uruguay, featuring no more than 13 teams, including hosts Uruguay, Argentina, Brazil, Belgium, Bolivia, Chile, France, Mexico, Paraguay, Peru, Romania, the United States of America, and Yugoslavia.

The United States finished third in that inaugural tournament, ahead of fourth-placed Yugoslavia, while Argentina finished as runners-up to champions and hosts, Uruguay. Argentina's Guillermo Stabile was the tournament's first ever top-scorer with a total of eight goals.

Soccer emerged stronger from the temporary global halt induced by the Second World War, with the restart of the World Cup hosted in Brazil, in 1950. A new soccer stadium was built in Brazil, the Maracana in Rio de Janeiro, which is still iconic and operational to this day. This was then the largest stadium in the entire world, officially seating 160,000 fans. In that tournament's final match between Brazil and bitter rivals Uruguay, attendance was reported to be over 200,000, a clear sign that the beautiful game of soccer had arrived on the global stage.

Partly as a result of its historic on-off relationship with some violent elements, soccer has largely been seen as a man's game, with the saying "football (soccer) is a man's game" often cited by patrons of the game seeking to affirm that it is indeed a contact sport. Women's football only earned similar recognition and following in the early nineties, when the very first Women's World Cup was held in China, in 1991. This inaugural Women's World Cup was won by the United States and the United States women's soccer team also went on to win the inaugural Olympic women's soccer event.

In the men's global soccer sphere, the sport's popularity gained traction as a result of its resemblance to modern-day warfare. By some considerable measure, the traditional (military and imperial) powers of the world saw the global soccer stage as a new way to demonstrate their might and assert their dominance. Purely from a soccer perspective however, the struggle for soccer supremacy continues to play out over two continents, Europe and South America. The Euro-zone leads the race as the most successful continent with 11 World Championship titles, while South America holds 9.

This says a lot about the strength of the South American zone because Europe enjoys what has long been seen as an unfair advantage by way of the number of team slots allocated the region. Europe is allowed 12 to 14 slots while South America has to make do with a maximum of five slots (in the modern games).

Brazil holds the most World Cup titles, with a total of five wins and two occasions during which they finished as runners-up. The Brazilians won their five titles in 1958, 1962, 1970, 1994 and 2002. Brazil's dominance on the international soccer stage gave rise to the saying which suggests that the British may have invented soccer, but the Brazilians mastered it.

The Brazilian national soccer team did more than their bit to popularize the game globally, bringing together artistic elements with organization to play the game and win "beautifully." The *Seleção*, as they are known, has long embodied what soccer is all about, bringing together the natural skill and flair associated with African players with the industrious organization and strategic prowess of the Europeans' approach to the game, to hold the most World Cup titles in history.

Germany also enjoyed a long-running period of on-and-off dominance on the global soccer stage, with four World Cup titles to their name (1954, 1971, 1990 and 2014). The Germans have also played in more finals than any other nation, finishing as runners-up on four occasions and bringing their total participation in finals to eight.

Italy is tied with Germany having also won the World Cup on four occasions (1934, 1938, 1982 and 2006). They have also finished as runners-up on two occasions.

Other nations to have tasted World Cup success include Argentina, who won it twice in 1978 and 1986, Uruguay who also won it twice in 1930 and 1950, while France, England and Spain have each come out on top once, in 1998, 1966 and 2010 respectively.

While fierce international rivalry and the emergence of individual superstars like Pelé and Maradona (among others), contributed to the rapid globalization of FIFA, club soccer also gained a lot of global traction, driven by the European club soccer revolution. What is now known as the UEFA Champions League is by far the top club soccer competition in the world, largely due to the Euro-zone's pioneering approach to beefing up their local squads with players from other regions and countries. More on club soccer in Chapter 4.

Perhaps the biggest parallel driving force of the explosive popularity of soccer was the game's introduction to television, with more of its significance to player transfers discussed in Chapter 4 as well.

In the 1954 World Cup hosted by Switzerland, one of the contributing factors to Germany's success as eventual World Champions was attributed to their soccer boots. Adidas emerged as the new German sports apparel and equipment company behind the national team's boots, which boasted screw-in stud technology and were thought to give the German players an advantage. Commercialization of the game in this way (sponsorship) came together with the marketing potential associated with a vastly growing interest in the game and its ever increasing accessibility through television. This leads us to the next chapter, which discusses how money changed the course of the history of soccer.

Chapter 3: The Effect of Money and Commerce on Soccer

The inevitable influx of money into the world's best loved game tells a story of two extremes, from the early days when arguably the greatest player of all time, Pelé, had to make do with a contract of only $10 per month. In stark contrast, average-rated players plying their trade today in the Barclays English Premier League earn a pretty standard salary of between £40,000 and £80,000, PER WEEK!

Many argue that money has generally had a negative effect on the game itself. The modern game of soccer is heavily commercialized, with players under increasing pressure to perform and deliver results over everything else. Soccer has become more about results than entertainment, although the institution very much still passes as entertainment.

An example of the immense pressure money has introduced to the game of soccer is that of a particular player from Africa (DRC), whose family sold their house to buy their budding football star a one-way ticket to Europe where he was scheduled to attend trials with a professional team. Professional soccer is nothing more than a decent-paying job for a lot of players, which is why players who genuinely enjoy the game will forever be remembered for their refreshing approach to the game. Again, one Ronaldinho (Ronaldo de Assis Moreira) comes to mind, a player who reached the pinnacle of the soccer world with his country (Brazil) and club (then Barcelona FC), going about his on-field business with a huge smile on his face.

While players will argue that the biggest soccer tournaments aren't in the slightest bit about the money ($30 million prize money for winning the FIFA World Cup), money has naturally played an extensive role in the development of the game. The decision to officially implement goal-line technology in the Brazil 2014 FIFA World Cup was undoubtedly partly influenced by the occasion where Frank Lampard's goal against Germany was disallowed (2010 FIFA World Cup held in South Africa). Although it wasn't the final and Germany went on to win comfortably, one could argue that a bad decision cost $30 million and also gave rise to yet another of soccer's derivative industries, the manufacture and sale of goal-line technology.

Several occasions clearly depict the influence money has had in altering the game, the most recent of which was the instant elevation of the English Club, Manchester City. It may have taken the team a season or two to get warmed up and find their stride, but ever since their ownership was taken over by the Abu Dhabi Group in 2008, Man City has effectively affirmed their place as one of the Premier League's top four teams. Since winning the league in the 2011/12 season, for the first time in 43 years, Man City, also known as the Citizens, the Blues or the Sky Blues, are now perennial challengers of the Barclays Premier League's top honors. They're beginning to find their feet in the continental club competition, undoubtedly seeking to use their financial muscle to turbo-boost their quest for Champion's glory.

Connect the dots and it's very easy to see that their recently-found wealth has seen them afford some of the world's top players, including the likes of Yaya Toure, Sergio Agüero, David Silva, Wilfried Bony and Edin Dzeko, among many others. This new money has since catapulted the club's fortune, serving as an example of just how much influence money can have on the evolution of the game.

On the other hand, clubs like Arsenal FC have consistently been able to turn a profit each season, with 2013/14 reserves in their coffers reportedly in the region of £120 million. Arsenal consistently manages to stay in the top four of the Barclays Premier League, despite their tag as a very frugal soccer club and enjoys a great global following nonetheless.

The relationship soccer has with money isn't always a positive one however. An example of this is Ivorian superstar Didier Drogba's premature exit from the Chinese Super League. The team with which he'd signed a two-and-a-half year contract, Shenhua Football Club, could no longer afford to pay his wages and that saw him leave for Turkish Team Galatasaray.

Between balancing sponsorships, gate-takings, player salaries and television rights remuneration, money has generally turned soccer into a game of financial muscle. Teams who can't afford to attract top talent are often disadvantaged in a number of ways, although some teams still manage to conquer the world without too much of an emphasis on spending big. Barcelona FC is the perfect example of this as they've been the best club soccer team for the last five years or so, with most of the talent in their roster made up of players who came through their development structures.

As it stands today (2015), the biggest ever transfer was that of a player named Garth Bale, who moved from Tottenham Hotspur in England to join Spanish giants, Real Madrid FC, for a world record fee of €100 million. This leads us away from the history of money in soccer and into a discussion of the history of player transfers.

Chapter 4: The History of Player Transfers

Television's growing accessibility coincided with a period in club football dominated by European giants, Bayern Munich, and left a legacy which still stands today. During this period of European club football domination (mid 1950s to very early 1970s), players and fans from other parts of the world were becoming exposed to European soccer, sparking a player-transfer tradition which is still very popular today.

Any modern soccer player active today dreams of landing a big-money move to the big European club football leagues, an ideal which continues to concentrate the world's soccer talent and strength in the Euro-zone. Further testimony to this is the emergence of leagues in other parts of the world, some of which can more than match the high salaries earned in Europe. Middle-Eastern Asia, for example, is in the midst of a growing soccer culture driven by the seemingly endless stream of oil money. An attempt to lure some of the world's best players to that part of the world are continuously failing more often than they succeed, with players choosing to look beyond the insane salaries and rather taking part in the built-up prestige of the top European club soccer leagues and competitions.

Our discussion of the history of soccer player transfers takes us back to Edson Arantes do Nascimento (Pelé), whose potential transfer to the richest club soccer leagues of Europe didn't happen. In order to keep Pelé's mesmeric talents accessible to local Brazilians, the government declared him a national treasure (1961), which effectively prevented him from any transfers to foreign-based clubs.

Going a little further back in history however, the concept of a soccer transfer is mainly attributed to England, after the FA's (Football Association) post 1885 introduction of player professionalization and subsequent player registration. Prior to this, players simply made an agreement with any club to play a series of games for the club, sometimes even just one game. Under the new regulations, players were required to register with just one club at the commencement of each season.

With the formation of the Football League in 1888, what is now common practice today met great resistance, when restrictions were placed on player transfers to negate richer clubs from trying to dominate by luring top players from competing clubs with their money. The law sparked some controversy, especially when viewed in retrospect because it also meant that players were effectively owned by the first club they registered with. Beginning the 1893/94 season, players couldn't register with any other team, even after the season they were registered in had concluded, unless they obtained permission from their "parent" club. It got worse before it became better though, because this meant that players weren't entitled to a salary, since they didn't hold a contract with the club they were originally registered with, should the club decide not to renew the annual contract.

1995 saw the introduction of the Bosman Transfer Law, which was named after a Belgian footballer, Jean-Marc Bosman. Bosman's story saw him win a legal battle which solved the conundrum he found himself faced with. As a result of the transfer laws which still stood since the 1893/94 season, Bosman's would-be new team (Dunkerque of France) didn't want to pay the £500,000 transfer fee his former Belgian club RFC Liege wanted, on grounds of the fact that his contract had expired. He didn't play during the dispute and had to make do with only 25% of his wages, after they were slashed due to his inactivity.

The European Court of Justice ruled in favor of players being freed up and allowed to move once their contracts expired. The Bosman Law has since given rise to some interesting and often controversial free-transfer moves, some of which are seen as betrayals by the fans of the teams the players left citing the Bosman Law. Notable Bosman law transfers include the likes of Sol Campbell, who moved from Tottenham Hotspur to bitter rivals Arsenal, Luis Enrique, who also moved to Barcelona from sworn enemies Real Madrid and Jay-Jay Okotcha, who moved from Paris Saint-Germain to Bolton Wanderers.

This leads us to the 2002 formation of the transfer window, which basically limited the exchanging and transfer of players throughout European leagues to two periods in each season, one which runs from the conclusion of the season up to the 31st of August, while the other plays out throughout the entire month of January.

The history of soccer player transfers wouldn't be complete without a list of highest transfers ever completed, which currently (2015) stands as follows (Top 10):

1. In 2013, Gareth Bale moved from Tottenham Hotspur to Real Madrid for a fee of €100 Million, which broke the previous record held by Cristiano Ronaldo's transfer from Manchester United to Real Madrid.

2. In 2009, Cristiano Ronaldo transferred from Manchester United to Real Madrid, for what was then a world record fee of €94.4 million.

3. In 2014, Luis Suarez joined Barcelona from Liverpool, for a fee of €94 million.

4. In 2014, James Rodriguez moved from AS Monaco to Real Madrid, for a fee of €79.5 million.

5. Tied in fifth-place are Angel Di Maria and Zinedine Zidane, both of whom moved for a fee of €75 million, from Real Madrid to Manchester United (2014) and from Juventus to Real Madrid (2001), respectively.

6. The sixth spot sees another tie, this time between Zlatan Ibrahimović and Raheem

Sterling, both of whom moved for €69 million. Ibrahimović moved from Inter Milan to Barcelona in 2009, while Raheem Sterling's 2015 transfer had him move from Liverpool to Manchester City.

7. In 2009, Kaká's (Ricardo Izecson dos Santos Leite) move from A.C. Milan to Real Madrid cost €65 million.

8. In 2013, Edinson Cavani moved from Napoli to Paris Saint-Germain for a reported fee of €64 million.

9. 2014 saw David Luiz move from Chelsea to Paris Saint-Germain, at a transfer fee of €62.2 million.

10. Luis Figo rounds up the list of the world's most expensive soccer transfers, with his €62 million move from Barcelona to rivals Real Madrid in 2000.

These figures make for some interesting reading, but if the list was adjusted for inflation, Cristiano would top the list as the world's most expensive player ever, followed by Gareth Bale in the second spot, with Zinedine Zidane completing the top three list.

Chapter 5: Other Interesting and Fun Soccer History Facts

1. The international soccer team said to have the worst luck in the world is the Netherlands. They have played in a total of three World Cup finals and finished as runners-up on each of those occasions.

2. Soccer was once illegal in Britain, due to its violent nature. In 1331, King Edward the Third of England passed laws to ban the game, while King James the First of Scotland also passed the same law in 1424. Queen Elizabeth the First took things a step further in 1572 however, enacting laws which could have soccer players imprisoned for a week after undergoing church penance. Soccer was only legalized again in England in 1605.

3. It's a myth that the United States has only recently discovered soccer. Oneida Football Club was the first ever soccer club formed anywhere in the world, beyond the borders of England. The club from Boston came into existence way back in 1862. The USA also participated in the very first FIFA World Cup

ever held, in Uruguay, 1930, finishing in third place.

4. The oldest player to have ever featured in the FIFA World Cup is Faryd Mondragon. The Colombian goalkeeper played against Japan in the 2014 World Cup in Brazil, at the ripe old age of 43 years. The oldest player to have ever SCORED in the World Cup however is Cameroonian Roger Milla, whose 1994 USA World Cup goal came at the age of 42 years, an amazing record in many respects since most "veteran" players playing beyond 35 (and 40 years) are goalkeepers.

5. Arguably the greatest player to have ever played soccer is Pelé, whose record 1281 goals came in 1363 games.

6. Some of the biggest David-versus-Goliath upsets in soccer include the USA beating England in 1950, North Korea kicking Italy out of the World Cup in 1966, and Albania shattering the hopes of West Germany qualifying for the European Championships held in 1967. The Germans were expected to win without much effort as they had already pummeled Albania 6-0, but Albania held on

for a goalless draw and Yugoslavia qualified ahead of West Germany. Other upsets (featuring "Davids getting ahead at the expense of many Goliaths"): Greece winning the European Championships in 2004, which were held in their country and Denmark winning the same competition twelve years earlier (Euro 92).

7. Former Manchester United goalkeeper, Alexander Cyril Stepney (Alex) was known for wearing his heart on his sleeve and never shying away from grilling his defenders if they didn't organize themselves properly. In addition to his unusual record as joint top scorer (he was a goalkeeper) at Christmas time (when United had been playing in the second division), Stepney shouted at his teammates so hard that he dislocated his jaw in the process.

Conclusion

Naturally, what makes for some of soccer's most interesting historical moments is as subjective as discussions concerning the game itself, like who the best player is/was, which is the best team to have ever played the game and even how the game should be played (purists versus results-at-all-costs patrons of the game).

There are many other ways through which the game of soccer has evolved, including the anatomy, intensity and frequency of the training methods, the evolution of the ball used in official matches, how the development of sports science has shaped the modern game and even the lifestyles led by professional soccer players and their families.

Throughout this book, I have sought to tell the history of the beautiful game of soccer from the point of view of some of the historical facts not usually discussed, so hopefully you've enjoyed reading about some aspects of the game that are completely fresh and are interesting additions to your knowledge of soccer.

By no means is this a comprehensive history, but hopefully you have gained a new appreciation for the game you probably already love so much. Hopefully, you will have a much more profound experience when you watch or play your next soccer match.

Finally, I'd like to thank you for purchasing this book! If you enjoyed it or found it helpful, I'd greatly appreciate it if you'd take a moment to leave a review on Amazon. Thank you!